SBP

EVERYBODY PLAY!

Group games and activities for young people

Written by
Ardnt Löscher

Edited by
Peter Klavora, PhD
School of Physical and Health Education
University of Toronto

Sport Books Publisher Toronto

Canadian Cataloguing in Publication Data

Löscher, Arndt
  Everybody play!

1st Canadian ed.
Translation of: Kleine Spiele für Viele.
ISBN 0-920905-22-6

1. Group games. I. Klavora, Peter. II. Title.

GV704.L6813 1990 796'.01'922 C89-094532-2

Distribution in Canada and worldwide by
Sport Books Publisher
278 Robert Street
Toronto, Ontario M5S 2K8

Printed in the United States

Contents

Foreword

Parents, P.E. teachers, coaches and instructors have long wished for a good, methodical collection of pick-up games and plays. This book is designed to meet their needs. Furthermore, this book will be of special relevance to elementary school teachers and workers at day care centers whose expertise in group sports and physical education is only rudimentary. Often working with very large numbers of children, and with only a very narrow range of exercises from which to choose, elementary school teachers and day care workers will benefit enormously from the exercises contained in this book.

Readers will find that this collection of games and plays is explained and illustrated in an easy to understand fashion. They are suitable for all groups—children, youth and adults— in kindergartens, summer camps, school yards, and parks. Anyone who is active and who is interested in physical activity will find this book relevant and beneficial.

To have a better overview of the individual games, they have been arranged according to their main characteristics. At the end of the book tables are provided to help the reader quickly find the appropriate game.

We hope that the book brings you many hours of pleasure.

Editor

Introduction

*We should
play more
often*

Games and plays presented in this book
can assist both young and old in general
physical development as well as in training
for many sports. Vacationers and athletes
alike will be so stimulated by the excite-
ment and challenge of these games that
the effort and physical exertion that they
require will go largely unnoticed.

*A lot can
be achieved
by playing
games*

These games consist of simple physical
activities which require no special prepara-
tion and can be varied in a number of
ways, and used for many purposes, warm-
up activities for athletes, active relaxation,
general fitness and developing co-ordina-
tion. In addition, they can provide a basis
for the cooperative activities of children
and youth, contributing in a very direct and
concrete way to the positive integration of
children and youth into society. Working
together and learning to acknowledge the
accomplishments of others are values
which are central to these games. Finally,
the games will serve to introduce simple
technical and tactical skills for athletes.

*Introduction
to the
content*

There are 51 versatile games contained in
this book, arranged according to their
principal activities. They are accompanied
throughout by variations, and summary of

the goals they are intended to achieve. Note the following in our descriptions of the games:

- *The number of participants/players* is generally the number for a group of players.
- *The size of the playing area* is only intended as a guide and should be adapted to meet local conditions.
- *The description and positioning of the players* and the object of game are explained in as practical terms as possible and simplified by means of illustrations showing key phases of the action of the game.
- *Game rules* are listed where they are required. Where readers desire to make changes or alterations in these rules, maintain the flow of activity.
- *The score* may be kept, if that appeals to the participants' desire to compete. For many of the games, however, it is not necessary to award points.
- *The variations* provide examples of possible changes that can be made to the general forms of the game and can be increased to include other possibilities.
- *The instructions and comments* for setting up are intended to ensure that the games are successful.

Playing should be an experience!

Any unfamiliar game must be presented in a consistent manner. The general procedure is as follows: (1) explanation; (2) demonstration; (3) trying it out. When participants understand the action and the rules, the game begins. Enthusiastic participation by all players indicates that a game has been set up properly. Problems in a game may mean that the rules need changing or that the explanations are not clear. Every time a game is played, the instructor's overall view is broadened, and participants improve their skills. The intended education and training effect is thereby achieved. For training purposes, a game may be repeated as often as the skills of the participants are measurably improved.

How to use the games

Each game in this book is found in the tables starting on pg. 92. The tables call attention to the suitability of each game for individual training goals. When the criteria given—such as participants' age and performance levels, time and space requirements, availability of equipment—are met, the game selected is suited to meeting the goals that have been set. Here are a number of very specific goals:

● *warming up and arousing enthusiasm* with sufficient and equal participation by all players (appropriate number of races, rounds, throws, matches, etc., without long pauses in between);

● *developing dexterity/coordination* with varied and more demanding movements (various types of motions, additional movement requirements, smaller playing area, varied types of throws, etc.);

● *developing speed* with fast body movements (sprints, reaction movements from various positions, powerful throws, etc., with sufficient number of pauses);

● *developing endurance* by increasing demands made on the body (larger playing area, increased number of races, matches, throws, etc., longer playing time, without any particular rests);

● *developing strength* by using heavier balls

(medicine balls), partner exercises, keeping specific body positions, etc.;

● *developing relaxation* by reducing mental or physical activity (less rigorous playing conditions such as more limited participation, longer rests, eliminations, simpler scoring, to name only a few).

Running games

Relay games (1-3)

1   Group races

Participants	6-40 in 2-4 groups.
Distance	10-20 m.
Equipment	Medicine balls (or other) for markers.
Description	The first player of each group runs a set distance and returns to the group. A group has won when all players have returned.
Rules and Distances	(a) Groups stand in parallel rows. Runners circle markers and return to their original places (Fig. a).
	(b) Groups stand in line beside one another. They run to a second line which runs parallel to starting line. They return to starting line in next race (Fig. b).
	(c) "Change sides": Two groups stand in line facing each other and trade places with other players after each race (Fig. c).
Score	Points are given for each race: The last group receives 1 point, the second-last group, 2 points, etc.
	No points are awarded an incomplete race.
Variation	Changes in starting and finishing positions (squatting, bench position, push-up posi-

tion, lying on back, etc.).
Changes in movement (hopping on one
leg, running on hands and feet, running
with hands joined, carrying partner, etc.).

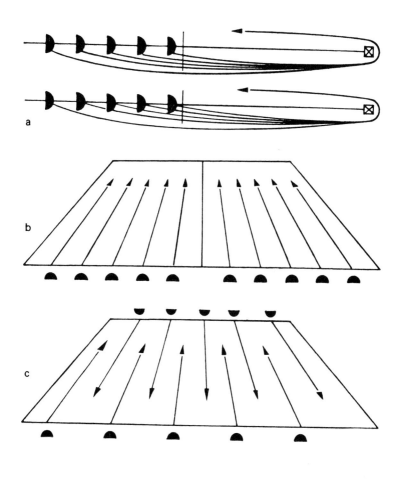

Comments

Disciplined participation is ensured when the movements are clearly described and scoring is exact. If races follow one another quickly, the end position is then the starting position for the next race. Start signal must be short.

d

e

2   Number races

Participants   6-40 in 2-4 groups.

Distance   10-20 m.

Equipment   Medicine balls (or other) for markers.

Description   The players of each group are given a number, and told to remember it. When the instructor calls out a number, players with this number start running, complete the predetermined distance and return to their original positions.

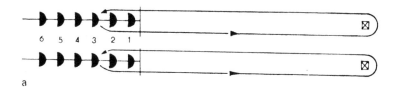

a

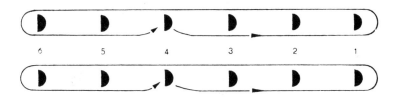

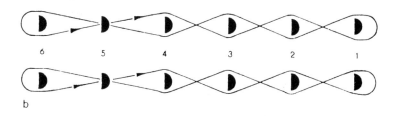

b

Rules and Distances	(a) The groups stand in parallel rows. The players run around markers (Fig. a).
	(b) Groups take up positions across a certain distance in open rows beside each other. The players run outside and around the group or back and forth between the players in a zigzag pattern (Fig. b).
	(c) Four markers form a rectangle. Each group forms a row behind a marker. The players run around the rectangle (Fig. c).
Score	Groups are awarded points after each race. The last runners receive 1 point, the second-last, 2 points, etc. No points are given for an incomplete race.
Variation	Changes in starting and finishing positions (squatting, sitting cross-legged, lying face down, etc.).
	Changes in movement (hopping on one leg, running on hands and feet, running backward, etc.).
	Adding movements (rolls, crawling through parts of crates, carrying balls, etc.).

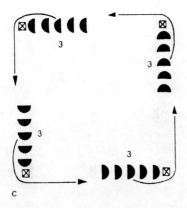

c

d

"Climbing up on top": Each group must run to a vaulting horse or crate, on which each player has to stand. If several players on the team are running at the same time, points are awarded only when all the players have climbed up on top.

Comments The fewer players in each group, the more often players' numbers can be called. By changing places, players compete against different opponents.

3 Relays

Participants 6-40 in 2-4 groups.

Distance Area: 10-20 m.

Equipment Highjump bars, etc., for markers; possibly balls, parts of crates, etc. for additional movement requirements.

Description The first runner from each group starts, runs the required distance, touches the next runner on the hands. The first runner then takes the last position in group. A group has completed its race when the last runner has returned to his or her place (or has reached the marker).

Rules
and
Distances

Backward relay: Each group stands behind a marker.
Players run around markers (Fig. a).

Cross relay: Each group divides itself into two halves standing at opposite ends of the playing area facing each other behind markers. Each runner runs to the marker on the other side (Fig. b).

Circuit relay: Four markers form a rectangle. Each group stands inside the rectangle behind a marker. The players run around the rectangle (Fig. c).

Score

Points are awarded for each race. The last group receives one point, the second-last, two points, etc. No points are awarded for an incomplete race.

Variation

Changes in movement (hopping on one leg, running on hands and feet, running backwards, etc.).
Performing additional movements (carrying partner, rolling and bouncing balls, climbing through obstacles, etc.).

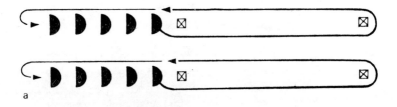

a

b

"Three-ball bumping race": Backward relay race with 2 teams; players carry 3 medicine balls (Fig. d). The players are allowed to bump into each other during the race. A player must pick up any balls that are dropped.

Comments

Instructions for clear explanations and demonstrations of the movements setting up should be clear and explicit to prevent players from executing movements incorrectly. Taking a player off after he or she has run around markers (see Fig. a and b) or after he or she has run around the group prevents the next runner from starting prematurely.

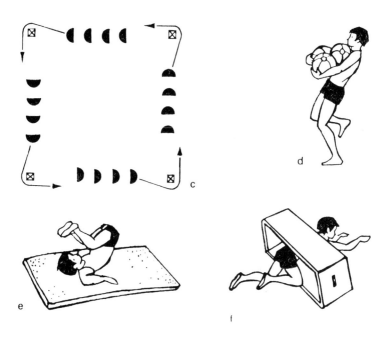

c

d

e

f

Position Games (4-16)

4   Dog house

Participants   15-30.

Rules   1-3 players fewer than half the players form a circle and open their legs in a straddle position. The players left over divide themselves up outside the circle.

Description   The players on the outside run around the circle. When a signal is given, each player tries to crawl into a "dog house" between the straddled legs of one of the players in the group. Any player left out has to run around again. The other players change places and those originally standing in the circle now run around it.

Score	Any player who cannot make a "dog house" loses a point. Which player has no minus points by the end of the game?
Variation	Changes in movement (hopping on one leg, running backward and sideways, running on hands and feet). The players in the circle also run, but in the opposite direction. Only when a signal is given do the players straddle their legs. *"Horse and rider":* The players in the circle are in bench position; players running around on the outside sit on top of them. Or, players in the circle are standing with legs spread firmly apart, and the players running around the circle jump on their backs in piggy-back style.

5   Come along - go away!

Participants	9-30.
Rules	Players join hands and form a circle, and then divide themselves up into groups of 2 to 5 behind each other. One player is outside the circle.
Description	The player outside the circle runs around the circle and calls to any one of the groups to join in running around, yelling: *"Come along!"* All the players in the group follow. But if the player calls out: *"Go away!"* they then run in the opposite direction back to their places. The last player back, including the player who calls, has to keep on running and call out to a

group as before.

Variation   Changes in movement (hopping on one
                leg, running on hands and feet, with player
                calling out deciding the movements).
                Changes in starting positions (squatting,
                bench position, sitting, etc.).
                After running around circle, players run to
                object in middle of circle (mat, chalk-drawn
                circle).

Comments   The game is more entertaining when the
                players calling out do not wait long and
                when all of the groups participate equally.

Tag games (6-16)

6   Ordinary tag

Participants   Up to 30.

Equipment   Ribbons, balls, etc., for the catchers.

Playing Field   Area:10-30 m x 20-50 m.

Description   About one-fifth of the players are the catchers and wear identifying markers (see equipment). Those left over are the runners and are chased by the catchers (Fig. a).

Score   (a) Catchers who tag runners are replaced by them. Which player makes the fewest tags?

a

(b) The catchers tag for a certain time (about 30 seconds) without being replaced. Which player takes the most runners off?
(c) A group of catchers tags until all runners have been taken off (runners caught must sit down). Which one (of the groups left) takes the least time?

Variation

Each catcher holds a ball in both hands and most touch the runners with it.

"Elephant tag": Catchers may tag only with arms in the position shown (see Fig. b).
Free-marker tag: On the playing field there are some medicine balls, mats, etc., which are the free markers: Players standing there cannot be taken off. At each free marker, however, there may be no more than 1 or 2 players. When a third player comes along, the first runner there must leave (Fig. c).

b

Small field tag: On a relatively small playing area, all the players or only the catchers must hop on one leg, run on their hands and feet or carry their partners on their backs.

Comments

In a specific playing area, increasing or decreasing the number of catchers can make the game more or less animated.

c

7   One player catches the other

Participants | 3-30.

Playing Field | Area: 10-20 m x 20-30 m.

Rules | The players are in groups of 2 or 3.
They all stay in the same area.

Description | (a) Two players take turns catching each other. After a player is caught, the new catcher lets the player run away.
(b) Three players take turns catching each other: first A-B, then B-C, then C-A, etc.; then in reverse order.

Variation | The catcher holds a ball with both hands and has to touch the runner with it.
On a narrow, marked-off field, each player hops on one leg, on both legs, or runs on both hands and feet.

8   Tag in pairs

Participants   8-40.

Playing Field   Area: 10-20 m x 20-30 m.

Description   Pairs of catchers join hands and tag individual runners (Fig. a).

Rules   If a pair releases its hands, the players may not tag.

Score   (a) One pair of catchers begins. The runners taken off then pair up and tag. Which runner is the last to be caught?
(b) Each time, a third or half the players form pairs and make up a team of catchers.
Which team catches all the other players in the shortest time?

a

b

(Players who are caught must go off to the side and sit down.)
(c) There is a specific number of pairs. Each runner caught replaces one of the catchers. Who takes the fewest players off during the entire game?

Variation

On a relatively small playing area the catchers link arms giving them a narrower reach (Fig. b). Of the 2 catchers, only one is allowed to take players off (the other player holds an identifying object, i.e., a ball).

9 Chain tag

Participants

6-20.

Playing Field

Area: from 15 x 15 m.

Description

Catchers link hands and form a chain. They tag the individuals running around.

Rules

Only the two end catchers with their hands free are allowed to tag. If the chain is broken, tagging may not be continued.

Score

(a) One catcher begins. Each runner tagged joins the catcher and plays. Which runner is not tagged until the end?
(b) In each game, a third or half the players form a catching team. Which team takes the shortest time to tag the other players?

Variation

If the playing area is small, runners may slip through the chain or break through it.

The chain of catchers is not to take off every player but rather to form a circle around the player.

10   Stop - go

Participants   6-30.

Playing Field   Area: 10-20 m x 20-40 m.

Description   A quarter to a third of the players are catchers and wear or carry an identifying object (ribbon, ball). The players left over are the runners. If tagged when told to *"stop!"* runner must squat (or sit down). The runner many only run again when touched by a free runner and told to *"go!"* The catchers form a team and have won when all the runners have been stopped.

Score   Several groups tag one after the other. Which groups of catchers win after a specified amount of time (1-2 minutes)?

Variation	*For 6-12 players.* Only one player is the catcher. If the catcher succeeds in tagging 2 or 3 runners before any is replaced, the catcher is replaced by one of the runners. *For 20-30 players.* Each time, 3 to 4 players tag for a certain amount of time (approx. 1 minute) together. How many players are stopped at the end of the minute?
Comments	The game is most interesting when the number of catchers is large enough that they succeed in tagging all the other players. Again, every free runner should take part in freeing tagged players. It goes without saying that honesty on the part of those tagged makes for a success-ful game!

11   Bogeyman

Participants	6-40.
Playing Field	Area: 10-20 m x 15-30 m.
Rules	1 to 5 players are the catchers and stand to one side of the field. They either wear or carry an identifying object (ribbon, ball). The players left over are the runners and stand on the opposite side.
Description	The catchers call out: *"Who is afraid of the bogeyman?* The runners answer: *"Nobody!"* The runners then try to reach a line on the opposite side of the playing area without being tagged.

(a) Each catcher who tags a runner is replaced by that runner. After players have changed sides a number of times, which player has not been tagged at all or has been the least number of times?
(b) Each catcher (or each group of catchers) tags several times. Which player (or group of players) tags the most?

Comments

Changes in movement (hopping on one leg, running on hands and feet, carrying partner).
On a narrow playing area only the catchers hop on one leg or carry with both hands a medicine ball with which to tag the runners. Only one of the catchers is allowed to tag; the others are allowed to hold on to the runners until they are tagged by the catcher.

12   Black - white (day and night)

Participants   6-30.

Playing Field   Area: 10 - 20 m x 20 - 40 m, with "out" area
behind both narrow lines.

Rules   The black and white teams stand 1-3 m
apart from each other in the middle of the
field.

Description   If the instructor yells: *"Black!"* or throws a
disc into the middle and it lands black side
up, the black team are the runners and
start running. The white team are the
catchers and try to tag them before they

reach the end of the field. When the
instructor yells: *"White!"* the game is
reversed.

Rules	Each runner may (or may not) be tagged by several catchers.
Score	Every time the catching team makes a tag, they score a point. Which team scores the most points in a given number of races?
Variation	Changes in starting position (squat, push-up position, lying face down, etc.). Changes in movement (hopping on one leg, running on hands and feet, etc.).
Comments	The distance between both teams in the middle is chosen according to the length of the playing area and the starting position so that the catchers tag all the players. After each race the catchers count up the number of tags.

13   Third man out

Participants	10 or more (fewer than 10 for last variation).
Description	Players form a circle in pairs 2 - 3 m apart. One catcher and runner are outside the circle. The catcher chases the runner around the circle. If the runner stands in front of a pair, the player on the inside of the pair is the third man out (see name of game) and

becomes the new runner. When a catcher tags a runner, they change positions.

Rules   A runner must tag no more than one (one half) round. Runners may not run through the circle. Runners may be tagged immediately.

Variation   The groups of players either squat or sit. Players in each pair stand *beside one another* or lie face down beside each other. The runner may stand either to the right or left or lie down. The outside players of each pair become the new runners. The catcher tags 2 runners at the same time. *Second man out:* The players stand, squat or lie individually in the circle.

14 The mother hen and the vulture (the hen and the hawk)

Participants   5-12.

Description   Players form a row and stand closely one
                      behind the other. Each player holds on to
                      the hips of the player in front. The player at
                      the front (the *"mother hen"*) spreads arms
                      out. A catcher (the *" vulture"*) stands across
                      from the row.

                      The vulture tries to go around the mother
                      hen to reach one of the players (the *"baby
                      chicks"*) behind. The mother hen prevents
                      the vulture from going past and runs, with
                      baby chicks behind, with the vulture. She
                      does not catch the vulture however.

Score   The vulture wins when he/she touches one
                      of the baby chicks or makes the row break
                      within a certain amount of time (approx. 30
                      sec.).

Variation	The mother hen places hands on hips, and the vulture reaches the last baby chick. The vulture is allowed to hold on to the baby chicks in order to reach the last one.
Comments	The game involves immediate vigorous movements and should not be started from complete inactivity. If all the players do not take a turn, the vulture and the mother hen should trade with players in the middle of the row, since those players are the least involved in the game.

15   Circle catch

Participants	5-10.
Description	The players form a circle and link hands. In a small circle, one player is chosen as runner; in a larger circle, 2 players standing approximately across from each other are chosen as runners. One player stands outside the circle and is the catcher.
	The catcher tries to reach one of the runners by going around the circle. Players in the circle try to prevent the catcher from doing so while continually running in the same direction as the catcher.
Score	The catcher wins when he or she reaches a runner or breaks the circle within a certain amount of time (approx. 30 seconds).
Variation	The catcher may hold on to players in the

circle. All the players go into squatting position.

Comments   The number of players between both runners should be such that the catcher can win.
The game should not be started from complete inactivity, since immediate vigorous movements are involved.

16   Head and tail

Participants   10-20.

Description   All the players form a line. Each player
puts hands on partner's hips in front. The
player at the front of the line is the *"head,"*
the player at the end is the *"tail."*

The head tries to reach the tail. If head
manages to do so within a certain period of
time, both players join the row in the
center. If unsuccessful, only the head joins
the center.

Ball games

Passing games (17-21)

17   **Pass-the-ball race**

Players   2-4 teams with 3-8 players.

Equipment   Identical volleyballs or medicine balls for each team.

Description	Each team forms circles of identical size. The circles should be large enough that there is equal throwing distance between the players. The ball is passed from player to player in the circle and goes around a certain number of times. The first team to finish wins.
Variation	Passing in sitting position or lying on stomach. Catching and throwing with one hand. Doing a complete circle with the ball. Playing with 2 balls at the same time. *Running:* the player who receives the ball runs with it round the circle and throws it to the next player.
Comments	If the circles are marked off, the players will not be creeping towards one another. Count the number of times the ball goes round; keep the ball high until the end of the game.

18   Chase ball

Players	6-16 in 2 teams.
Equipment	2 identical volleyballs.
Description	The players form a single circle, such that a player takes turns standing in the circle. Each team has a ball and both throw it from player to player in one direction at the

same time until a player misses the ball.

Variation   The ball is passed with players sitting down
                 or lying on stomach. Catching and throwing
                 is done with one hand.
                 Each player does a complete revolution
                 with the ball. In a fairly large circle the ball
                 is passed with the feet.

Comments   Each player has to stand so as not to
                 obstruct the other team's players. The
                 better the players can catch and throw, the
                 farther apart they can be and the smaller
                 the number of players in the circle to keep
                 the game exciting.

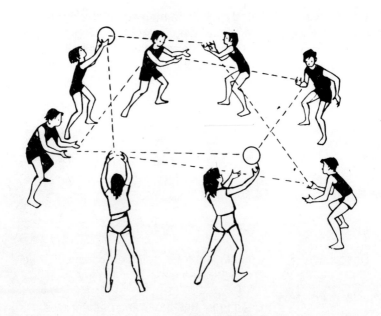

---

19   Tiger ball

Players   4-8.

Equipment   Volleyball or medicine ball.

Description   The players form a circle approx. 4-8 m wide. One or 2 players are in the center as the "tigers."

The players on the outside throw the ball back and forth to each other. The tigers try to touch or catch the ball.

Rules   The players on the outside may not leave their places. The tigers are free to move where they please.

(a) A tiger who touches the ball is replaced by the player who last played the ball. How often does each player replace the tiger?
(b) Each player is the tiger once. After how many throws or how often within a certain number (15 - 20) of throws does the tiger reach the ball?

Variation

Each player may hold the ball for only 3 seconds. The players outside sit or lie on their stomachs, and the tiger has to catch the ball.
In a somewhat larger circle the feet are used to throw the ball.

Comments

If players' places on the outside are marked off, it is easier for them to stay in one spot. The circle should be only so big that the tiger can still win. (For players with good ball control ratios of 3:1 and 4:2 are the most suitable).

20   Snatch ball

Players

3 on a field.

Equipment

Volleyball or medicine ball.

Playing Field

Area: marked-off area approx. 5 x 5 m.

Description

Two players inside the area throw the ball back and forth to each other. The third player tries to intercept (to "snatch") the ball.

Rules	All 3 players may move anywhere they want inside the field. The catcher may also run outside the field.
Score	(a) The player who snatches the ball away is replaced by the last player to touch the ball. How often does each player snatch the ball? (b) Each player must snatch the ball once. After how many passes between the other players does the player snatch the ball? How often does the player reach the ball in a certain number (15-20) of passes?
Variation	The ball is rolled or passed indirectly (by bouncing on the ground. On a slightly larger field the ball can be thrown with the feet. *One on one:* One player bounces the ball on the ground continuously, while the other player tries to touch it (see Fig.). Several pairs play together on the same field.

21   Group (snatch) ball

Players	4-12 in 2 groups.
Equipment	Volleyball or medicine ball.
Playing Field	Area: 6 x 6 m to 20 x 20 m, according to number of players and form used.
Description	The players in one group throw the ball back and forth until the other team catches it and plays it in the same manner.
Rules	*Handball style:* The player with the ball may not be touched or tackled; the ball may not be taken from player's hands. Holding the ball, the player may take up to 3 steps and stand still for up to 3 seconds. *Basketball style:* The player with the ball may not be touched, but the ball may be taken from hands. Holding the ball in hands, the player may take up to 2 steps and hold it indefinitely while standing still.
Score	(a) Which team makes the most consecutive passes? (b) Only when a team has made 5-10 passes in a row does it receive a point. Which team scores the most points? (c) Which team keeps the ball for the longest time?
Variation	The ball may not be controlled (dribbled). The ball may be passed indirectly only by bouncing. The ball may be thrown or caught with one hand only. The game is played according to soccer

rules.

Group snatch ball on 2 fields: The playing area is divided into halves. In each half are equal numbers of players from each team. The ball may only be passed within a half. If a player from the other team snatches it away, player must throw it to the players on own team on the other half. These players throw the ball back and forth until an opponent snatches it away, etc. Players change roles after a predetermined length of time.

Comments

A player on each team may be given the task of counting the number of passes. The smaller the playing area or the more players, the more difficult passing becomes. The larger the playing area and the fewer the players, the more difficult intercepting becomes.

Ball games with target shooting (22-26)

22   Target ball

Players   6-20 in 2 teams.

Equipment   For every 1-2 players, a volleyball for throwing and several medicine balls or bats for targets; gym bench or carton lid for mat.

Playing Field   Area: 12-20 m long, according to players' throwing strength. Targets are collected in the center.

Description   Both teams stand behind the end lines facing each other.

         The players throw volleyballs at the targets until all have been knocked off or cleared away.

Score	Which team accumulates the most points? (Each target knocked off counts as a point, or each time surface is cleared the better team receives a point.)
Variation	The balls are thrown with the weaker arm, in a sitting or lying position, through the legs with both hands or are kicked with the feet.
Comments	To make an exciting game the throwing style used and the number of targets should determine the distance from the targets. If there are too few balls for the number of players, teams should be divided into catchers and receivers and alternated continually.

23   Drive ball

Players	6-20 in 2 teams.
Equipment	Solid medicine ball or basketball for driving ball; 5-10 medicine balls or volleyballs for throwing.
Playing Field	Area: 8-15 m x 8-15 m, according to the players' throwing strength. Goal lines run 1-2 m before end lines.
Description	Teams stand behind end lines facing each other.
	The driving ball is placed on the center line. Both teams throw balls at it until one of them succeeds in driving it across the

opponent's goal line.

Rules   The balls may not be withheld (hoarded).
                 Each team retrieves the balls from its own
                 half of the field.

Comments   Gym benches turned sideway and placed
                 on the end lines prevent players from
                 stepping over the line. If there are only a
                 few balls available for throwing, use
                 players as ball retrievers.

24   Ball under cord (ball under net)

Players	8-20 in 2 teams.
Equipment	2-8 volleyballs or medicine balls; volleyball net, gym bench, ribbon or cord to mark height.
Playing Field	Area: approx. 10 x 20 m. The net or cord is stretched across the middle of the area (or benches are placed across the middle) and is 0.5 - 1 m off the ground; throwing lines are marked on both sides 1 - 3 m from cord. Each team is on half the playing area.

Description	Each team tries to throw the balls under the obstacle to the area behind opponents' end line while preventing other team from doing so.
Rules	A team receives a point for each mistake the other side makes. *An error is made when* (1) the ball crosses the end line; (2) a player, throwing, hits the cord, throws over or steps over throwing line. (Throwing into the net is not counted as a mistake.)
Score	A game lasts for a specific time (5 - 10 minutes) or until a certain number of points (20 - 40) is reached.
Variation	The balls are kicked with the feet (suitable only when using a volleyball). Saves are made by (or without) using the arms. In each half of the field, medicine balls or bats are piled on top of one another. If they are toppled, the other team receives an additional point, or more.
Comments	The size of the playing area, the height of the obstacle, and the number of balls should be chosen so that players can make several successful throws in a short time. If more than 3 balls are being used, a scorekeeper must stand on each end line. If teams frequently withhold (hoard) balls, possession of the ball should be limited to 3 seconds. When there are a large number of players, each team can be divided into defence players and throwers.

25   Ball over cord (ball over net)

Players

4-16 in 2 teams.

Equipment

1 or 2 volleyballs or medicine balls; volleyball net or cord.

Playing Field

Area: 4 x 8 m to 10 m 20 m.
The net or cord is stretched across the middle of the area within the players' reach. When a cord is used, throwing lines are 1 m away on each side.
A team plays on half the area.

Description

Each team tries to throw the ball over the net or cord onto the ground on the other side, while preventing the other team from doing so in its half.

Rules

A team receives a point for each error the other team makes. After an error, the ball is played from its position at that time.

The player who catches the ball must throw it back over head (or may pass it to a partner). If 2 balls are being used, each ball must be thrown to opponent immediately.

An error is made when (1) the ball hits the ground in the playing area; (2) a player throws it out, at the cord, under it or steps over the line when shooting. (Touching the net is not counted as a mistake.)

Score
A game lasts for 5-10 min. or until a certain number of points (10-20) are scored.

Comments
Equal participation by all is ensured if players trade front and back positions.

26   Line ball (drive ball)

Players
4-10 in 2 teams.

Equipment	Volleyball, medicine ball or rounders ball (for children).
Playing Field	Area: 15-20 m x 50-100 m for a volleyball: 10-15 m x 30-50 m for a medicine ball, depending on throwing style used and players' throwing strength.
Description	Both teams stand in the middle of the playing area one throwing length apart.
	Players take turns throwing ball back and forth. By throwing hard, each team tries to force its opponents back over their goal line.
Rules	(1) The ball is thrown from where it lands. Players throw balls in turn. A player who catches the ball may take 3 steps forward and throw out of turn. (2) The ball is thrown from where it was caught in the air, stopped on the ground or left lying. The player who stops the ball must throw it.
Variation	The ball can be hit with the foot (on the first throw) or kicked on the ground (Fig. a). A volleyball can be hit with either the hands or fists (Fig. b).

a

b

Ball games with elimination of players (27-30)

27   Adding up hits (each player against the other)

Players   Minimum of 8.

Equipment   1 or 2 volleyballs.

Playing Field   Area: **approx. 15 m x 5 m**, larger or smaller according to number of players and players' throwing strength.

Description   The ball is thrown into the field. The player catches it tries to hit another player with it. Each player plays alone and counts own hits scored.

Rules   The player with the ball has to stand still. A player who catches the ball has not been hit.

Variation	The player with the ball may chase the other players while continuing to bounce the ball on the ground (suitable for a few players in a large area and with players whose throwing strength is more limited). Only indirect throws (when ball touches the ground first) count as hits. At the end of the game, anyone who has been hit is eliminated.
Comments	When number of players is high, 2 balls are used. Possible extra rule: Both balls are not to be thrown at one player at the same time! The player who fails to score is the loser!

28   Speed ball

Players	3-16.
Equipment	Volleyball or medicine ball.
Playing Field	Area: circle or rectangle (size according to ball style used and players' throwing strength).
Description	Some of the players are distributed outside and around the circle. (In rectangle formation, players stand behind 2 opposite lines.) The other players go into the playing area.
	Players on the outside have the ball and try to hit the players running away from the ball on the inside. The ball is played quickly back and forth

from side to side.

Rules

Each direct hit is counted. If ball remains lying on the field, players on outside retrieve it. Players on the inside may not touch it intentionally.

Score

(a) With a few players only 1 player is on the field. How often is player hit during a certain time (1-2 min.)?
(b) Team match. Half the players are on the field. How long does it take for the players on the outside to score a certain number of hits (10-20)? With elimination, how long does it take for all the players on the field to be eliminated?

Variation

The ball is thrown underhanded either with both hands or when thrown heftily. Outside players lie on their stomachs in the circle and throw the ball with both hands.

Comments

With extra ball, when the ball rolls a considerable distance and has to be retrieved, it may be replaced by another ball which is ready close by.

29   Chase ball

Players	6 in 2 teams.
Equipment	Volleyball or medicine ball.
Playing Field	Area: approx. 15 x 15 m, even larger for volleyball.
Description	Both teams - *the hunters* and *the hares* - are in the same playing area. The hunters run after the hares, pass the ball back and forth and try to hit the fleeing hares. When the game is finished, players change roles.
Rules	Every direct hit counts. The hunters may not run with the ball in their hands. The hares may not intentionally touch a rolling or lying ball.

Score	(a) All hares remain on the field. How many hits do the hunters score within a certain time (approx. 2 min.)?
	(b) Hares that are hit are eliminated. How long does it take for all the hares to be eliminated?
Variation	Hares run onto the field individually from one of the sidelines. When a hare has been hit 2 or 3 times, the next one starts. How much time do the hunters need to hit all the hares? The hares run from a sideline one at a time through the playing area to the opposite side and back again. Each time one completes his run, the next one starts. Hunters try to hit every hare on the field as often as possible. How many hits do they score altogether? On a fairly small playing area the hunters can only execute hefty throws.

30   Two-fielder ball

Players	4-20 in 2 teams.
Equipment	Volleyball or medicine ball.
Playing Field	Area: 5 x 10 m to 10 x 20 m, divided in half.
	Size of playing area depends on ball used and players' throwing ability.
Description	Inside players from each team have 2 on their own half of the playing field. There are also 1-3 outside players who stand behind the opponents' half.

Each team tries to eliminate the inside
players on the other team with the ball.

Rules

Each player is allowed to eliminate. Only
direct hits count. If an inside player catches
the ball, the hit does not count. Players
may not touch or cross over onto opposite
side.

Score

(a) All the players on the inside stay on the
field. Which team scores a certain number
of hits (10-20)?
(b) Anyone hit becomes an outside player.
Which team eliminates all the players on
the other team?

Variation

The players on the outside may throw from
all 3 sides.
Place a vaulting horse, behind which
players may hide in the middle of each
half.

Comments

When the number of players is high, equal
participation by all players is ensured by
having outside players racing to score
points.

Simple sports games (31-35)

31   Roll ball

Players   6-12 in 2 teams.

Equipment   Volleyball or small medicine ball.

Playing Field   Area: approx. 15 x 20 m. The goals are 3-4 m wide, with or without a goal line about 2 m around each goal.

Description   The ball is moved by rolling it on the ground. Both teams try to put the ball in the other team's goal.

Rules   Roll ball is played to handball rules:
The game begins with the ball at the center of the field. The ball may be rolled as far as desired with one hand and held by both hands on the ground for up to 3 seconds. Ball may not be intentionally played with the feet. The ball may be taken from opponent only if other player is not holding it with both hands. The opponent may not be pushed or held.
Only one player may defend each goal. The opposing team may not step into the goal. When a team breaks a rule, the other team is entitled to a free throw. When a ball is thrown out, the other team is entitled to a throw-in. Opponents must remain 3 m away from the player commencing play, free throwing or throwing in.

Variation   For children on a relatively small playing field: the entire width of the baseline serves as the goal. 2 or 3 players may defend the goal area.

Comments   The size of the playing area, the ball style used and team numbers should be established so that passing and shooting on goal can be freely done. Since body position in this game is strenuous, play should not last for more than 10 minutes. Where the number of players permits, 3 or 4 teams should play tournament-style games of approx. 5 min. in length. The constant deep trunk bends required by the game should be balanced, especially among children, by backward stretching movements (see tiger ball in lying position).

32   Scuffle ball

Players	8-16 in 2 teams.
Equipment	Medicine ball. With small number of players, 2 gym mats serve as goals.
Playing Field	Area: approx. 15-20 m x 30-40 m.
Description	Both teams start at their goal line in order to capture the ball. The ball may be carried and passed forward. The teams compete to put the ball behind the goal line or set it down on opponents' mat.
Rules	The ball may be held, thrown or rolled in any fashion but may not be played with the feet. The player carrying the ball may be tackled or held until he loses control of the ball.

When players are piled up, a deciding throw is made (ball is tossed into the air between a player from each team). After a rule infraction, opponents have a free throw; if ball goes out, opponents get a throw-in. Kicking, pulling and tripping, etc. are not permitted. Anyone playing unfairly is removed from the game.

Variation

As in rugby, the ball may be carried only forward (to the opposite goal line). The ball may be passed only back (towards the team's own goal line).

33   Crab soccer

Players

8-16 in 2 teams.

Equipment

Medicine ball, possible 2 gym benches.

Playing Field

Area: 8-13 m x 12-15 m. Baselines or gym benches placed on the field are the goals.

Description

Each player moves face up on all four and plays the ball with feet. Each team tries to put the ball in the other team's goal.

Rules

A kick-off in the middle of the playing area begins the game. The ball may not be played intentionally with the hands and arms. It should not be held between the feet.
Players may not take both hands off the ground at the same time.
Each time a rule is broken, the other team has a free kick, each time the ball is

knocked out, the other team has a free kick.

Comments

Given the great strain placed on the arms, a game should not last any longer than 10 minutes. Where the number of players permits, 3-4 teams can play tournament-style games, 5 min. long.

34   Burn ball

Players   8-20 in 2 teams.

Equipment   Rounders ball and bat (50-80 cm-long slat); 4 stakes for markers; medicine ball for burn base.

Playing Field   20 x 30 m to 30 x 40 m outdoors, on the edge of an area measuring 50 x 70 m. The edges of the field are the bases.
Hitting area is on one edge of the field.
Burn base is approximately 5 m in front of the hitting area.

Description   One team begins as the batters, the other as catchers. The hitters go into the hitting area; the catchers divide themselves up in the field.

Players on the hitting team take turns and hit the rounders with the bat (Fig. a) far into or across the playing field. The player who has hit the ball may run, as long as the ball is in play - from the right base in the hitting

a

area and around the field to the left base in the hitting area. Any player who has run may hit again. The players on the catching team catch the ball and play it quickly to the burn base; the ball is only in play from the time it is hit to the time it touches the burn base (Fig. b).

Rules

A hit counts when the ball is in the field or falls to the ground. A player may run on his or her own hit and also on the hit of the next player. The player stops at every base on the field and waits for next hit. A player who has left a base on a disallowed hit must go back to the base.

If a runner is caught between 2 bases when the ball touches the burn base, the runner is "burned." Player is eliminated until catchers and hitters switch rolls, or

b

until the catching team receives a point, at which time the player returns to the hitting field and may hit as the last batter up.

The team at bat scores a point for each run and for every ball hit over the field ("wide hit").

The team catching scores a point for each ball caught with one hand and for each "burned" runner, if the game is being played without elimination (see above).

Score   Each team is at bat or catching in the field either for a certain time (10-15 min.) or for a certain number or rounds (3-5).

Variation   Hitting a volleyball with the feet. (Same as shot by goalkeeper.) Hitting a volleyball with the hand (on a smaller playing field; in a spacious gymnasium).

Comments   A safe distance must be kept from the player at bat. A wide bat is necessary initially. A player who misses may hit a second time.

35   Bounce volleyball

Players

4-8 in 2 teams.

Equipment

Volleyball or similar type of ball; plastic ball; gym benches or cord for obstacle in center.

Playing Field

Area: 6 x 12 m to 10 x 20 m, divided in half by an obstacle 30-40 cm high.

Description

To begin the game, the ball is served with the fist or the flat of the hand and is bounced so that it hits the ground on the serving side and then goes over the middle barrier. The team on the other side may let the ball bounce once and may bounce it twice on their own half. By the third bounce the ball must be hit back over the middle in the same way that it was served (touching the ground first on serving side). Each team tries to hit the ball so that the other team makes a mistake.

Rules

A team scores a point for each error made by the opposing team.
An error is made when (1) the ball touches the obstacle in the center, a player or the ground outside the playing area; (2) the ball is played on one side more than 3 times or more than twice in a row by one player; (3) after bouncing, the ball hits the ground a sec. time on the same side or is hit underhand up into the air.
The team that faults has the next serve. Ball may be served from anywhere on the field.

Score

A game lasts for a specific time (10-20

min.) or until certain number of points are scored (20-30).

Variation   The game may be introduced to children in a simpler fashion: each time the ball is bounced, it may bounce a second time.

Comments   For inexperienced players, competition is advisable only after game is practised a sufficient number of times. Two-man teams are best if everyone is to take an active part in the game. For 3 and 4 man teams, the game may be set up so that each player may hit only once.

Strength and dexterity games

Tugs-of-war and pushing matches (36-42)

36 Tug-of-war

Players   Groups of 2-4.

Description   Two players each stand across from each
                       other on a 3-5 m strip. Players grab each
                       other by the left (right) hand (Fig. a).

                       Each player tries to pull opponent over the
                       line behind.

Variation   Players grab each other by both hands,
                       with a helper behind each player (Fig. b).
                       Players stand with their backs to one
                       another and grab each other with both
                       hands (Fig. c and d).
                       Players are on all fours and grab each
                       other by the right (left) hand. Each player
                       tries to push opponent over or to pull
                       opponent out of position.

a

b

c

d

37   Pushing match

Players
Groups of 2-4.

Description
Two players each stand between 2 lines 3-5 m apart and grab each other by the upper arms (Fig. a).

Each player tries to push the other player back behind own line.

Variation
Players stand back to back and lock arms together (Fig. c).
Players are on all fours and put their right (left) shoulders against each other (Fig. b).
Players sit back to back.
Two teams, with arms locked, stand in 2 chains across from each other.

Comments
Game is fruitful when 3-4 players of approximately the same strength fight against each other. The farther apart the lines, the longer and more substantial the matches.

a

38   Ringed circle

Players   2-5 around a circle.

Equipment   About 2-4 medicine balls or 5 bats.

Description   Players form a circle around the piled-up medicine balls, around the bats or a chalk circle approx. 1 m in diameter. Players grab each other by the hands.

Players try to push and pull the other players - each player against the other or 2 teams against each other - in order to topple the bats or balls or to pull player across the circle (Fig. a).

b

c

Score	The player who knocks over the balls or the bats or steps into the circle receives a minus point or is eliminated.
Variation	Stepping with both feet at the same time into a slightly larger chalk circle is counted as an error. Six to eight players make a ring around a pile of medicine balls; they lock their arms (Fig. b).
Comments	Even with a large number of players, the chalk circle should be small enough that the players can still jump over it. Breaking the hand grip frequently should be avoided.

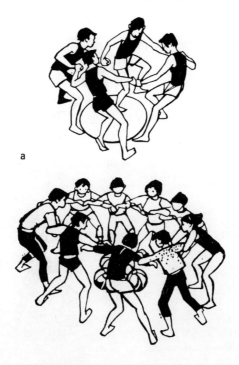

a

b

39 Throwing player out

Players 2-10.

Playing Field Area: marked-off surface of 3-5 m in diameter.

Description All the players stand within the playing field.

After a signal is given, players try to force each other off the field.

Rules Anyone touching the ground outside the field with any part of the body is eliminated. Kicking, pulling or carrying partners is not allowed.

Score Players can fight as individuals one against another or as teams. Who is the last player left on the field?

40   Breaking out

Players   6-12.

Description   Some of the players join hands to form a circle, and the remainder stand inside the circle.

After a singnal is given, the players inside the circle try to "break out."

Score   (a) 2 to 4 players are inside the circle. Who is the first player to break out of the circle?
(b) Team match: half the players are inside the circle. How long does it take for all the players to break out?

Variation   3 players grab hands. Without releasing this grip, each player tries to push between the others.

41   Jumping out of the circle

Players

10-20.

Description

All the players lock arms to form a circle.

Players stand close to one another. When a signal is given, they start to run backward. Anyone who falls out of step and breaks the circle is eliminated or receives a minus point.

Variation

The players form a circle with their backs to the middle.

42 Stiff man

Players	10-15.
Description	One player lies down with body stiff and with arms held tightly at the sides. The rest of the players sit with their legs locked in a close circle around the player and push arms out towards that player.

The *"stiff man"* falls and is continually pushed back and forth by the seated players. |
| Score | Anyone who fails to push the "stiff man" away or from his or her right side has to go into the middle. |

Balance fights (43-48)

43   Cockfight

Players | Group of 2-6.

Playing Field | Area: marked areas 3-5 m in diameter.

Description | Two players are in the middle of the playing area. Their arms are folded across their chests and they hop on one leg. Each player tries to push the other from the area or onto the other foot either by pushing or by dodging the opponent's moves (Fig. a).

Score | Who wins most rounds when each player meets all the others? Who wins all rounds when losing players are eliminated?

Variation | Players join one or both hands with their partners and push and pull each other (Fig. b).
Each player grabs raised ankle, and both

a

players try to break the other player's grip by using free arm to push the other player (Fig. c).

Comments

Players not taking part should be used as referees. Care should be taken to put equal strain on both legs.

b

c

44 Squat fight

Players

Group of 2-6.

Playing Field

Area: marked-off surfaces 3-5 m in diameter.

Description

Two players squat in the middle of the playing area facing each other and put palms forward.
Each player tries to push the other from the playing arm by pushing against opponent's hands and shoulders or by avoiding opponent's shoves. Players can also try to

topple their opponents or force them onto their hands (Fig. a).

Score

Who wins the most rounds when each player meets all the others? Who wins all his/her matches when players who lose are eliminated?

Variation

Each or only one player holds a ball in front of chest, with or on which players push. Each player holds onto ankles. Opponents push each other with their shoulders (Fig. b).

Comments

Players not involved in the match should be used as referees.
Players may not hold each other with their hands. Players should not be pushed while fingers are spread out (possible injury).

a

b

45   **Fighting on the line**

Players

Group of 2-4.

Description

Two players stand facing each other with one foot behind the other so that all 4 feet are in a line. Both players keep one hand open in front of them (Fig. a).

Each player tries to upset the other's balance, forcing opponent to leave the line by hitting opponent's hand or by trying to avoid opponent's efforts.

Variation

Players stand facing each other with feet parallel and both arms in front. They try to push each other off balance (Fig. b).
Players are in squatting position.
Players stand on top of an overturned gym bench.

a

b

46   Foot fight

Players   Group of 2-4.

Description   Two players sit facing each other not using
their hands and place soles of feet together
in the air (Fig. a).

Each player tries to push the other out of
position by pushing against the soles of the
feet or by trying to avoid opponent's efforts.

Variation   Players fold arms in front of their chests
(Fig. b).

a

b

47   Arms away!

Players   Group of 2-4.

Description   Two players face each other in push-up position.

Each player tries to make the other fall by pulling away supporting arm (Fig. a).

Variation   Players try to slap opponent's hand on supporting arm (Fig. b).

a

b

48   Feet away!

Players   Groups of 2-4.

Description   Two players face each other with their
hands behind their backs (Fig. a).

Players attempt to step on opponent's feet.

Variation   Players place hands on opponent's shoulders (Fig. b).
Two or more players grab hold of each
other by the hands and form a circle.

a

b

Wrestling matches (49-51)

49   Leg locks

Players

Groups of 2-4.

Description

Two players lie on their backs next to each other head to hip and lock arms.

After a signal is given, each player raises "inside" leg, locks legs with opponent and tries to force opponent to roll backward by pushing down on leg.

Score

Who wins the most matches when each player fights all the others?
Who wins all the matches when losing players are eliminated?

Comments

If possible, matches should be carried out on a soft surface. Care should be taken that equal strain is applied to both sides of the body.

50   Lifting

Players   Groups of 2-4.

Description   Two players face each other.
               The player tries to grab and lift opponent
               off the ground.

Variation   Players stand back to back and lock both
               arms around each other.
               Players stand with their backs to each
               other. After a signal is given they turn
               around.

51   Fighting for the ball

Players   Groups of 2-4.

Equipment   Medicine balls or large volleyballs.

Description   Two players stand facing each other and
               both have hands around one ball.

After a signal is given, each player tries to wrestle the ball from the other.

Variation

One player holds the ball; the other tries to take it away within a certain length of time (10-20 seconds).

Application of games to fitness development

On the following pages all games contained in this book have been arranged in table form according to their main characteristics. These tables are provided to help the reader quickly find appropriate games designed to stimulate specific fitness factors.

Table Application of Games to Fitness Development.

Game No.	For Warming Up	Developing Coordination	Developing Speed
1	•	• with variations	•
2	•	• with variations	•
3	•	• with variations	•
4	• with variations	• with variations	•
5	• circle with few groups	• with variations	•
6	• scoring a	• with variations	• scoring c
7		• with variations/ small playing fields	•
8	•	•	—
9	•	•	—
10	•	• on small field	•
11	•	• with variations	• wide field
12	•	• with variations	•
13	—	• with variations	•
14	•	• in small groups	•
15	•	•	•
16	•	• in small groups	•
17	• small teams/ with variations	• with variations	—
18	• same as No. 17	• with variations	—
19	• scoring b	•	•
20	• scoring b	•	
21	•	• on small field	•
22	• using many balls	—	—
23	• same as No. 22	—	—

Developing Endurance	Developing Strength	For Fun and Relaxation
—	• using specific lead-up activities	—
—	• same as No. 1	with agility tasks
•	• same as No. 1	same as No. 2
—	—	—
—	—	—
• scoring b	—	•
• on large field	—	• in threes and fours
• on large field/ scoring b	—	—
• on large field/ scoring b	—	• scoring a
• on large field	—	—
—	• using specific	—
—	—	—
—	—	—
—	—	•
•	—	• in large groups
•	—	—
—	• with heavy balls/ great throwing distance	
—	• same as No. 17	
—	—	• with variations
—	—	• with variation
•	—	—
—	• great throwing distance	•
—	• same as No. 17	•

Table Application of Games to Fitness Development.

Game No.	For Warming Up	Developing Coordination	Developing Speed
24	•	•	—
25	• on large field/ two balls	• using small teams	• large field/ two balls
26	• following rules 2	—	—
27	• using two balls	• on small fields	—
28	• scoring b	• scoring b	—
29	• scoring a	•	• variations
30	• scoring a	•	—
31	•	•	—
32	•	•	•
33	•	•	—
34	•	•	•
35	• using small teams	—	—
36	• with variations	—	—
37	• with variations	—	—
38	•	•	—
39	•	•	—
40	• scoring b	—	—
41	• with variations	—	—
42	—	—	—
43	• scoring a	•	—
44	• scoring a	•	—
45	—	•	—
46	•	•	—
47	•	•	—
48	• with variations	•	—
49	• with variation	•	—
50	•	—	—
51	—	—	—

Developing Endurance	Developing Strength	For Fun and Relaxation
—	• same as No. 17	•
• throwing with jump	• using heavy balls/ throwing with jump	•
•	•	• follwing rules 2
—	—	•
• scoring b	• using heavy balls	• with variations
• scoring b	—	• scoring b
• using small teams	• using heavy balls	• scoring a
•	•	—
•	•	—
•	•	—
•	—	•
—	—	•
—	•	—
—	•	—
•	•	•
•	• scoring b	•
—	•	• scoring a
—	•	•
—	•	•
•	•	• scoring b
•	•	• scoring b
—	—	•
—	—	•
—	•	•
—	—	•
—	•	—
•	•	—
—	•	—